बात अभी बाक़ी है...

Unfinished Conversations

Ghazals

Dr. Sanjeev Chaudhary

ALEPH

ALEPH

ALEPH BOOK COMPANY
An independent publishing firm
promoted by ***Rupa Publications India***

First published in India in 2025 by
Aleph Book Company
161-B/4, Gulmohar House,
Yusuf Sarai Community Centre,
New Delhi 110049

ISBN: 978-93-6523-369-8

1 3 5 7 9 10 8 6 4 2

Printed in India

For my parents,
Sh. Ishwar Dass Chaudhary and Smt. Krishna Chaudhary

Contents

Author's Note

Poetry, to me, is not merely an expression but a way of conversing with the soul—a dialogue with life, love, and the silent emotions that often remain unspoken. As a cardiologist, I have witnessed life in its most vulnerable moments, where every heartbeat narrates a story of hope, struggle, and resilience. Over the years, these experiences have shaped my understanding of human emotions and have found voice in the form of these ghazals.

This book, a collection of my heartfelt ghazals, is an attempt to capture the subtleties of love, longing, fear, and the search for meaning. Each ghazal reflects a fragment of my journey—sometimes contemplative, sometimes rebellious, and at times, profoundly spiritual. The interplay of Hindi and Urdu words, blended with English translations, is intended to make these emotions accessible to a wider audience while preserving the soul of classical poetic traditions.

No creation is ever complete without the support of those who stand beside you. I owe my deepest gratitude to my wife, Dr. Savita Chaudhary, a remarkable paediatrician and a woman of extraordinary grace and strength. Her unwavering encouragement and understanding have been the bedrock of my creative and professional journey. I also extend my heartfelt thanks to my son, Dr. Shivin Chaudhary, whose entrepreneurial spirit and belief in me have been a constant source of motivation.

This book is a tribute to life's unfinished conversations—stories that continue to evolve with every breath we take.

ख़ुद से मुलाक़ात

Reflections of the Self

Exploring identity, internal conflicts, and self-realisation

मुझसे मेरा तारुफ़ करा दे

ऐ ज़िंदगी, किसी रोज़ मुझसे मेरा तारुफ़ करा दे
आख़िर मैं चाहता क्या हूँ, मुझे तो बतला दे

हर फ़तह के बाद तलाशता हूँ नयी मंज़िलें
शायद कोई मुक़ाम मुकम्मल[1] सुकून दिला दे

कुछ शग़ल[2] लाज़मी[3] है इस बेमक़सद जहां में
इश्क़-विश्क़ बहाना है, कोई मेरे यार को समझा दे

बार बार मेरे अज़्म[4] का इम्तिहान न ले मेरे दोस्त
जाने कौन सा लम्हा मुझे मेरी नज़रों से गिरा दे

ऐ ख़ुदा, अपने तौर तरीक़ों पे भी तो गौर फ़रमा
कहीं ऐसा न हो तू इक मुख़्लिस[5] मुरीद[6] गवाँ दे

है ज़्यादा सुकूँ क़ुर्बत[7]-ए-यार में, सजदा वहीं कर दिया
गुस्ताख़ी ये नादानिस्ता[8] नहीं, कोई ख़ुदा को समझा दे

Let Me Meet Myself

O life, one day, introduce me to myself,
Tell me what I truly want, make me aware.

After every victory, I seek new destinations,
Perhaps some milestone will bring me complete peace.

Some indulgence is necessary to survive in this monotonous world,
Love is just an excuse—someone, please make my beloved understand.

My friend, don't test my resolve again and again,
Who knows which moment might cause me to fall from my own sight.

O God, reflect on your own ways,
Lest you lose a sincere devotee, in your trials.

There is more peace in the closeness of my beloved, I bowed right there,
This audacity is not unintentional; someone explain it to God.

इक दिन

ख़ुद को समझ जाऊँ इक दिन
ये पसोपेश सुलझाऊँ इक दिन

थोड़ा साथ मिल जाये मुझे अपना
ख़ुद को फ़तह कर जाऊँ इक दिन

कभी बेवज़ह भी ख़ुश रहा करो
आईने को समझाऊँ इक दिन

किस क़दर शुक्रगुज़ार हूँ ज़िंदगी
तहे दिल से बतलाऊँ इक दिन

तमाम दुनिया की परवाह जाने दूँ
अधपकी ग़ज़लें सुनाऊँ इक दिन

न ख़लिश, न कश्मकश हो ज़हन में
यूँ ही बेसाख़्ता[9] मुस्कुराऊँ इक दिन

One Day

If only I could understand myself one day,
Solve this confusion and find my way.

If I find a little company of my own,
I'd conquer myself, and finally be known.

Sometimes, be happy without any reason,
I'd make the mirror understand the season.

How grateful I am to life, truly,
From the bottom of my heart, I'd tell it fully.

Let go of the world's concerns,
I'd express all my half-written rhymes.

No longing, no struggle in my mind,
I'd smile freely, unburdened and kind.

डर लगता है

(सामाजिक)

जब से होने लगा हूँ बेपरवाह
डर लगता है
हो न जाऊँ ज़माने की तरह
डर लगता है

तमाम उम्र जब सलीक़े से गुज़ार दी
अब मन क्यों होने लगा गुमराह
डर लगता है

नज़रें चुराता हूँ हमेशा अपने आप से
कभी तो सामने होगा आईना
डर लगता है

वक़्त कटा सारा मदह परस्ती[10] में
क्या जवाब दूँगा जब पूछेगा ख़ुदा
डर लगता है

पुरसुकून हूँ वहशत के आलम में भी
कहीं बदल तो नहीं गया मैं पूरी तरह
डर लगता है

Facing the Mirror

Since I've become indifferent,
I fear,
What if I end up like the world,
I fear.

I've spent a lifetime in order and decorum,
Now, why does my heart feel so lost?
I fear.

I always avoid facing myself,
One day, the mirror will confront me,
I fear.

All this time, I've lived in materialistic pursuits,
What will I say when God asks me about my actions?
I fear.

I remain at peace, even in the realm of madness,
Have I changed completely, deep inside?
I fear.

डर लगता है

(भावनात्मक)

जब से होने लगा हूँ बेपरवाह
डर लगता है
हो न जाऊँ बिल्कुल तुम्हारी तरह
डर लगता है

वो बेवफ़ा ताउम्र सुकून को तरसे
कहीं कुबूल न हो जाये मेरी ये दुआ
डर लगता है

बर्दाश्त से बाहिर है अब शिद्दत-ए-जज़्बात
क़रीब न आ जाना तुम बेवजह
डर लगता है

अब मैं ख़्वाहिशें बयाँ नहीं करता
कहीं तुम मान न लो मेरी इल्तजा
डर लगता है

वक़्त कटा सारा सजदे में महबूब के
क्या जवाब दूँगा जब पूछेगा खुदा
डर लगता है

तुमसे बिछुड़ के भी ज़िंदा हूँ अब तक
कहीं बदल तो नहीं गया मैं पूरी तरह
डर लगता है

Lost in Fear's Embrace

Since I've become indifferent,
I fear,
What if I turn out to be exactly like you?
I fear.

The unfaithful one should be cursed,
What if my prayer is accepted?
I fear.

The intensity of my feelings is beyond endurance,
Don't come near me for no reason,
I fear.

I no longer express my desires,
What if you accede to my requests?
I fear.

All my time has been spent in devotion to my beloved,
What will I answer when God questions me?
I fear.

Even after parting from you, I'm still alive,
Have I completely changed?
I fear.

बात अधूरी सी

The Incompleteness of Love

Longing, betrayal, distance, and the ache of unfinished love

बात अभी बाक़ी है

कुछ देर अभी और बैठो कि बात अभी बाक़ी है
हजारों करवटें हैं नसीब में कि रात अभी बाक़ी है

कुछ देर और ज़िंदा रहता तो नाम लबों पे आ जाता
जवाब की तलाश में कुछ सवालात अभी बाक़ी है

समझा दूँगा तुम्हें भी बेवफ़ाई का सबब लेकिन
ज़रा ठहरो, मुझसे मेरी मुलाक़ात अभी बाक़ी है

हलचल हुई मेरे जनाज़े में जो उसका ज़िक्र आया
जिस्म फ़ना था मगर रूह में जज़्बात अभी बाक़ी है

ख़ुदा नाराज़ है, मैंने महबूब को ख़ुदा माना मगर
महबूब मुझे अपना माने, ये क़रामात अभी बाक़ी है

हैराँ है सितमगर भी मेरी हिम्मत देखकर 'संजीव'
बर्बाद हो चुका है फिर क्यों औक़ात अभी बाक़ी है

Unfinished Conversations

Stay a little longer, for the conversation is still unfinished,
Thousands of turns of fate await—the night is far from done.

If I lived just a little longer, your name would be on my lips,
In search of answers, many questions remain unanswered.

I will explain to you the cause of betrayal, but,
Wait a moment, first let me introspect.

There was a stir at my funeral when your name was mentioned,
The body was gone, but emotions lingered in the soul.

God is displeased for I considered my beloved as divine,
But my beloved must see me as human; that miracle is yet to happen.

The oppressor is astounded at my strength,
Though I am ruined, my worth remains.

अब वो पहले से हम नहीं

(Thoughts of an Ageing Person)

न तुम अब तुम हो,
हम भी अब पहले से हम नहीं।

ये तक़ाज़ा उम्र का है,
और इस दर्द का मरहम नहीं।

इतनी तिशनगी[11] कैसे तस्कीन[12] हो,
आग़ोश[13] में मेरे अब वो दम नहीं।

इत्मिनान से क़रीब चले आओ,
शदीद[14] अब वो पहले से हम नहीं।

बज़्म[15] सूनी है मेरी तलाश-ए-मुरीद में,
नग़मों में मेरे अब वो तरन्नुम[16] नहीं।

सबब नहीं, मंसूबा नहीं, मक़सद नहीं,
ज़ीस्त[17] ये मौत से कुछ कम नहीं।

आरज़ू है, जुंबिश[18] का नामोनिशाँ नहीं,
इससे भारी दूसरा कोई ग़म नहीं।

Not the Same Anymore

I am not the same anymore,
You have also changed.

This is the corrosive effect of increasing age,
This wound can't be soothed.

How can your desires be fulfilled?
My embrace is not that passionate anymore.

You can come closer without any fear,
I am not that intense anymore.

The whole gathering is bereft of true disciples,
My musings don't strike a chord anymore.

No purpose, no aim, no motive is left,
This life is worse than death.

Aspiration is present, but there's no drive left,
There is no bigger regret in life.

हाथ हम बढ़ा न सके

ज़माने को यक़ीन-ए-मोहब्बत हम दिला न सके
निगाहें बोलती नहीं और इज़हार हम करा न सके

कोशिशें संजीदा[19] थीं मेरी अहद-ए-वफ़ा[20] में
उन्हें एहसास न हुआ और हम जता न सके

उम्रभर मलाल रहेगा नासमझ तवक्कुफ़[21] का
क़रीब से गुज़रा वो मगर हाथ हम बढ़ा न सके

मेरे जनाज़े में शहर की सब गलियाँ वीरान रहीं
मसरूफ़[22]-ए-खुदपरस्ती[23] रुतबा हम कमा न सके

इक छत के नीचे मीलों का फ़ासला क्यों है
ये अपने दिल को कभी हम समझा न सके

वादा था पर्दादारी का मगर एक तबस्सुम[24] पर
हाल-ए-दिल कह डाला कुछ भी हम छुपा न सके

न मालूम था इतना महंगा है बाज़ार-ए-आरज़ू
बर्बाद हो कर भी ये क़ीमत हम चुका न सके

बाद मुद्दत के, हम थे, वो थे और तन्हाई थी मगर
शोर-ए-इल्ज़ाम में हाल-ए-दिल हम सुना न सके

बावजूद तजाहुल[25] के बार बार इज़हार-ए-बंदगी[26]
चाह कर भी अपनी ये लत हम छुड़ा न सके

A Promise Unfulfilled

The world didn't believe in love as we did,
Yet, our eyes were silent, we couldn't express it, we hid.

I was sincere when I vowed loyalty,
You never felt it, and I couldn't show it openly.

A lifetime of regret remains for my foolish pause,
You came so close, but I was unable to pursue my cause.

At my funeral, the streets were empty,
Because of my selfishness, I couldn't earn the esteem.

Why the distance under one roof, why the divide?
I could never explain it to my heart, no matter how I tried.

I promised to stay veiled, but with one smile,
I revealed my heart, and couldn't hide it for a while.

I never knew how expensive the market of desire could be,
I lost a fortune but could neither pay nor set myself free.

After long years, it was me, it was you, and loneliness too,
But amidst the noise of accusations, I couldn't convey the truth to you.

Despite my disregard, I expressed devotion,
No matter how much I wished, I couldn't break this obsession.

तेरा नाम लिया ही नहीं

ख़्वाहिशों का कारवाँ तेरे दर से आगे बढ़ा ही नहीं
और क्या माँगते तेरे सिवा कुछ सूझा ही नहीं

सबूत तमाम थे मेरे पास अपनी बेगुनाही के मगर
तेरा ज़िक्र आ गया तो सफ़ाई में कुछ कहा ही नहीं

उँगलियाँ उठती ज़माने भर की जो मैं पूरी दास्ताँ सुनाता
सारा फ़साना कह डाला तेरा नाम लिया ही नहीं

दो निगाहें नम हुईं, महफ़िल में जब मेरा नाम आया
तरीक़ा ये इज़हार-ए-इश्क़ का, समझ आया ही नहीं

तमाम उम्र बदहवास गुज़ार दी बस तलाश में
और क्या ढूँढना है 'संजीव', ये पता ही नहीं

Search Without an End

The caravan of desires never moved beyond your doorstep,
And what else could I ask for, when nothing else seemed right but you?

I had all the proof of my innocence, yet,
When your name came up, I didn't say a word in my defense.

If I had told the whole story, accusations would've been rife,
I shared the entire tale, but never uttered your name.

Two eyes grew teary when my name was mentioned in the gathering,
This strange way to express love, I never understood.

I spent my whole life in a frantic search,
And what was I searching for, 'Sanjeev'? I never knew.

तस्वीर-ए-सजदा

Dialogue with the Divine

Questions to God, spiritual turmoil, and existential negotiation

तुझ पर भी इल्ज़ाम है

ऐ ख़ुदा मेरे क़रम[27] में कुछ सुकून शामिल कर दे
या तारीफ़ न बख़्श या तारीफ़ के क़ाबिल कर दे

इश्क़ ग़र गुनाह है तो तुझ पर भी इल्ज़ाम है ऐ ख़ुदा
इस क़दर बनाया उसे, कोई कैसे न क़ुर्बान-ए-दिल कर दे

जुर्म-ए-मोहब्बत में वो भी बराबर का शरीक़ था
ख़ुदाया उसका भी तो जीना मुश्किल कर दे

मैंने ये कब कहा कि वो फ़क़त[28] मेरा हो जाये मगर
उसके फ़साने में मेरा ज़िक्र हो, इतना तो हासिल कर दे

जाने कब से तलाशता हूँ शब-ए-इत्मीनान
कभी ख़्वाब में आकर मेरी नींद मुकम्मल कर दे

I Am Not the Only One to Be Blamed

Oh God, please grant some peace in my deeds,
Either withhold praise or make me worthy of it.

If love is a sin, then You are equally to blame,
For You created her in such a way that one can't help but surrender one's heart.

In the crime of love, she, too, was a partner,
If You are impartial, then make her life as difficult as mine.

I never said she should only belong to me,
But let my name be a part of her story—that much I ask for.

I don't know for how long I've been searching for a tranquil night,
But if You could visit me in my dreams, make my sleep complete.

ज़रूरत क्या थी

(After a Life-threatening Illness)

मैं तो इशारे भर में सब कहा मान जाता ऐ ख़ुदा
इतना पास बुला के समझाने की ज़रूरत क्या थी

मुझे तो कभी भी अपनी हस्ती का गुमां ना था
फिर औक़ात दिखाने की ज़रूरत क्या थी

सजदे में मेरे कुछ कमी रह भी गई थी अगर
सारे ज़माने को जताने की ज़रूरत क्या थी

माना कि तेरे क़रम के बिना महज़ ख़ाक हूँ मगर
इस बेदर्दी से समझाने की ज़रूरत क्या थी

जब इक पल में धुआँ होनी थी सारी शख़्सियत
इतना साज़-ओ-सामान जुटाने की ज़रूरत क्या थी

What Was the Need?

I understand every gesture, O God,
Why did you need to explain it so harshly?

There was never an air of haughtiness about me,
So, why the need to show me my place?

If there was any flaw in my submission,
What was the need to show it to the whole world?

I acknowledge I am but zilch without your grace,
Why did you teach me with such cruelty?

When my entire existence is so fleeting,
What purpose did all materialistic gains serve?

पहचान की तलाश

उम्र सारी गुज़र गई इत्मीनान की आस में
आईने से जा उलझे गिरेबान की तलाश में

रुतबे की जुस्तजू[29] ने भी क्या क्या रंग दिखाये
अक्स अपना लुटा दिया पहचान की तलाश में

मैं और मेरा वजूद आमने-सामने हैं खुदाया
ये कैसा मक़ाम आ गया ईमान की तलाश में

कभी रास्ता बदल दिया और कभी ख़यालात
सफ़र दुश्वार हुआ अनजान की तलाश में

परिंदे ने खुद अपने पर काट दिए 'संजीव'
क़फ़स[30] नसीब हुआ आसमान की तलाश में

Search of an Identity

A lifetime passed in hope of tranquillity,
I had to quarrel with the mirror in search of my own collar.

The pursuit of status revealed its many hues,
I squandered my own reflection in search of an identity.

I and my very existence stand face to face, O Lord,
What situation is this I've reached in search of faith?

Some changed the path, some changed their mind,
The journey turned arduous in search of an unknown.

The bird clipped its own wings, 'Sanjeev',
And found a cage in search of the sky.

ज़माने की बात

The World and Its Wounds

Social unrest, injustice, and collective grief

मौत का सबब

(My Take on Pollution)

इस गर्द-ओ-गुबार में ग़ज़ब का अदब है
है हर सीने में जलन, ख़ामोश हर लब है

कैसे महफ़ूज़ रहेंगे नर्म जज़्बात इन फिज़ाओं में
ज़र्रे-ज़र्रे में ज़हर, हर नफ़स[31] मौत का सबब है

तेरे शहर की जानिब न आता तो शायद ज़िंदा होता
यहाँ साँस लेने वालों का यही अंजाम मुंतख़ब[32] है

फ़ना होना तो लाज़मी है कुछ हलचल तो करो
रफ़्ता-रफ़्ता यूँही ख़त्म होने का क्या मतलब है

फ़िजूल लफ़्फ़ाज़ी[33], ख़्वामख़ाह तोहमतें
मैं हूँ या तुम हो, गुनाहगार सब के सब हैं

Cause of Death

In this dust and chaos, there is a strange form of respect,
Every chest burns, yet every lip is silent.

How will soft emotions stay safe in these surroundings?
Every particle is poisoned, each breath a cause of death.

Had I not come to your city, I might still be alive,
This is the fate of those who breathe here—inevitable and chosen.

Annihilation is inevitable, but at least make some effort,
What's the point of fading away bit by bit?

Empty words, baseless accusations,
Whether it's me or you, we're all guilty in the end.

इंसान दरबदर हो गया

मज़हबी जुनून में आदमी इस कदर खो गया
हिमायत में जानवर की, ख़ुद जानवर हो गया

दहशतपसन्दों[34] की भीड़ है हर चौराहे पर
जिसने दरवाज़ा खोला वो बेघर हो गया

सुनता जो रहा मैं सबकी कहानियाँ
आँसुओं से पैराहन[35] तरबतर हो गया

मैंने भी कुछ सीनों में घोंप दिया ख़ंजर
पर क्या मेरा दर्द कमतर हो गया?

कुछ मकानों में अब चराग़ नहीं जलते
तमाम गली मोहल्ला मुंतशर[36] हो गया

इनाम बंट रहे हैं, किसने कितने चाक[37] किए
शहर-ए-बेचराग़[38] में इंसान दरबदर हो गया

ख़ामोश देखता रहा क़त्लेआम होते हुए
ख़ुदा पर भी ज़माने का असर हो गया

A City of Despair

In the madness of religious zeal, man has lost himself,
In defending animals, he became as savage as them.

There's a crowd of extremists at every corner,
Whoever opened the door, ended up homeless.

I listened to everyone's stories,
And my clothes were drenched in tears.

I, too, thrust a dagger into some hearts,
But did it lessen my pain?

Some homes have been darkened forever,
The entire street and neighbourhood have been shattered.

Awards are being handed over to murderers,
In the city of despair, humanity is now lost.

He silently watched the massacre unfold,
Even God seems affected by the world's chaos.

नीयत का इम्तिहान

हर बार मेरी नीयत का इम्तिहान लेते हो
कितनी आसानी से मेरा कहा मान लेते हो

मेरी आँखें दग़ाबाज़ी करती होंगी शायद
इक नज़र में दिल का हाल जान लेते हो

इश्क़ ख़ुदा से भी बदस्तूर हो सकता है
क्यों बेवजह किसी ग़ैर का एहसान लेते हो

बड़े दिलकश लगते हैं गिले शिकवे तुम्हारे
खुदाया किसी बहाने तो मेरा नाम लेते हो

इस कदर तन्हाई की आदत हो गई है
बुझा के चराग़ों को साये से इंतक़ाम लेते हो

जब ज़िक्र आता है मेरी हक़ अदायगी का
तमाम मजबूरियों का दामन थाम लेते हो

Test of My Intentions

Each time, you test the depth of my intent,
So easily, you believe every word I've sent.

Perhaps my eyes betray me,
With a single glance, you read my heart.

Love can be as pure as devotion divine,
Then why, without cause, accept favours unrefined?

Your grievances seem so endearing,
O God, at least you speak my name.

You have become so accustomed to solitude,
Extinguished the lamps and take revenge on the shadows.

When there is discussion about my rights,
You cling to every excuse of worldly constraints.

यही सिलसिला जारी है

दिन-रात जो ज़हन में बेक़रारी है
क़ुसूरवार सिर्फ़ तेरी समझदारी है

ख़ुद को जीत कर चैन मिले शायद
ताउम्र हर शब करवटों में गुज़ारी है

अब कोई वादा न करना ख़ुद से
जाने कब से यही सिलसिला जारी है

उधार की ख़्वाहिशें, बेवज़ह की ख़लिश
किस हुनर से तुमने ये ज़िंदगी सँवारी है

पस-ए-आईना ढूँढते रहते हो वो शख़्स
सुकून जिसको हर क़ामयाबी पे भारी है

कितना भी साज़-ओ-सामान जोड़ ले नादाँ
ख़ुदा के घर इक दिन सबकी बारी है

The Weight of Restlessness

The restlessness that fills your mind day and night,
Only your wisdom is to blame for this plight.

Perhaps peace will come by conquering myself,
But a lifetime has passed, spent turning in restless night.

Now, make no promises to yourself,
This unbroken cycle has been going on for ages.

Borrowed desires, an unwarranted ache,
How have you shaped your life, for heaven's sake?

Across the mirror, you keep searching for that soul,
For whom peace is more valuable than any success.

No matter how much you gather,
One day, everyone has to leave everything here.

इश्क़ की आवाज़

Echoes of Ishq

Romantic intoxication, spiritual love, and surrender

ज़िंदगी का नशा

तेरी क़ुर्बत का सुरूर है, वाबस्तगी[39] का नशा है
ज़रूरत नहीं मैक़दे की, मुझे ज़िंदगी का नशा है

क्या बयाँ करूँ सबब उसकी बेवफ़ाई का
ख़ता मेरी नहीं, उसे आवारगी का नशा है

बस गिरेबान झाँकना था वफ़ा की तलाश में
हर सूँ समंदर है मगर, उसे तिशनगी का नशा है

पहले कभी न थी ये जुंबिश इस महफ़िल में
ज़र्रे-ज़र्रे को आज तेरी मौजूदगी का नशा है

हैराँ है वो वहशत[40] में मेरा इत्मीनान देखकर
बावफ़ा मेरी रूह को बंदगी का नशा है

Intoxicated by Life

The intoxication of your nearness, the addiction of attachment,
I need no winehouse, for life itself is my true obsession.

How can I explain the reason behind your betrayal?
It's not my fault—you were intoxicated to waywardness.

It was enough to look within, in search of commitment,
Though there are oceans around, she is intoxicated with thirst.

Never before was there such stir in this gathering,
Every speck of dust today feels your presence, in every whispering.

They are amazed by the peace they find in my wild gaze,
For my loyal soul is intoxicated with devotion's sweet embrace.

तेरे बिन

तेरे बिन मेरी गुस्ताख़ियाँ अपनाता कौन
तेरे बिन मेरी बेक़ैदगी[41] गले लगाता कौन

बिखरे बिखरे से रहते थे मेरे ख़यालात
तेरे बिन मेरे अशआर[42] मुझे समझाता कौन

तुम हो तो मकाँ मेरा माहताब सा चमकता है
तेरे बिन मगर दरीचों[43] में चाँद सजाता कौन

अपने चेहरे पे मुखौटा पहना रहा मैं उम्र भर
तेरे बिन मेरे अश्क़ लबों से लगाता कौन

ज़िंदगी फूल है, धनक[44] है, शबनम भी है,
तेरे बिन मगर ये सब मुझे बताता कौन

इक लौ काफ़ी है स्याह रात मिटाने को मगर
तेरे बिन मुसलसल[45] ये शमा जलाता कौन

डूब जाता अक्सर मायूसी के दरिया में
तेरे बिन मुझे साहिल[46] पे खींच लाता कौन

हौसलाअफ़ज़ाई से सारा जहाँ जीत लेता
तेरे बिन मगर मेरा सर कांधे पे सजाता कौन

Without You, Who?

Who would embrace my defiance, if not you?
Who would welcome my idiosyncrasies, if not you?

My thoughts were always scattered and broken—
Without you, who would help my verses find meaning?

When you're around, my home glows like moonlight,
But without you, who would hang the moon in my windows?

I wore a mask on my face all my life—
Without you, who would kiss away my hidden tears?

Life is a flower, a rainbow, a drop of dew—
But without you, who would help me feel its wonder?

One flame is enough to chase away a dark night,
But without you, who would keep that flame burning?

I often drown in the sea of despair—
Without you, who would pull me back to the shore?

With encouragement, I could conquer the world—
But without you, who would place my head on their shoulder?

फ़िर से जवाँ हो जाता हूँ

जब भी तेरे ख़याल में खो जाता हूँ
भरी अंजुमन[47] में तनहा हो जाता हूँ

मेरी संजीदगी[48] के सब क़ायल थे मगर
तेरे आते ही जाने क्या हो जाता हूँ

तेरा आग़ोश या ख़याल आग़ोश का
इस उम्र में फिर से जवाँ हो जाता हूँ

ज़िक्र जब हुआ जमाल-ए-यार[49] का
रक़ीबों[50] से भी हमनवाँ[51] हो जाता हूँ

कभी तग़ाफ़ुल[52] कभी निगाह-ए-मोहब्बत
अक्सर तज़ब्जुब[53] के दरमियाँ हो जाता हूँ

फिर तलाशूँगा क़ाबिल-ए-ऐतबार सनम
दिल में ख़्वाहिश लिए फना हो जाता हूँ

Youthful Once Again

Whenever I lose myself in thoughts of you,
In the midst of a crowd, I feel so few.

Everyone admires my sobriety but,
The moment you arrive, I don't know what I become.

Your embrace or the thought of your embrace,
Even at this age, I feel youthful once again.

When talk is of the beauty of my beloved,
I cannot but concur, even with my rivals.

At times indifferent, at times a gaze of love full-blown,
Often, I find myself lost, every sense shredded and torn.

I'll seek a lover worthy once more of my trust,
And in that pursuit, lose myself I must.

शमा जलाते रहिए

दोबारा फिर मिले न मिले, जश्न-ए-ज़िंदगी मनाते रहिए
पत्थर पिघल जाएँगे खुद ब खुद, प्यार जताते रहिए

बहुत दिन हुए दहलीज़ पर आहट नहीं सुनी तुम्हारी
कुछ वक़्त निकालिए, ख़्वाब में आते जाते रहिए

शायद किसी लम्हा उन्हें हमारा भी ख़याल आए
उम्मीद की चौखट पे बदस्तूर[54] शमा जलाते रहिए

बेरहम दुनिया है हुज़ूर, कुरेदने में माहिर है
यूँही अपने ज़ख़्म सरेआम न दिखाते रहिए

इश्क़ से ख़ूगर[55] हुआ तो बर्बाद हो कर रहेगा
कितना भी दुनियादारी का सबक़ सिखाते रहिए

Keep the Flame Burning

Whether we meet again or not, keep celebrating life,
The stones will melt on their own, just keep showing love's light.

It's been days since I've heard your footsteps by the door,
Take some time, and in dreams, come and go once more.

Perhaps in a moment, they'll remember us too,
At hope's doorstep, keep the candle burning true.

The world is ruthless, my dear, skilled at prying deep,
So, don't display your wounds for all to see or keep.

If you become too used to love, you'll be ruined,
No matter how many worldly lessons you've been given.

यादों का लिहाफ़

कोशिशों के बाद भी जब ग़मों ने साथ न छोड़ा है
तलाश-ए-सुकूँ में तेरी यादों का लिहाफ़ ओढ़ा है

जब भी देखा है तेरा नाम लिखा किसी पन्ने पर
नज़रें चुराकर हमने, हरबार वो सफ़ा मोड़ा है

तू आबाद रहना अपनी मौक़ा परस्ती के साथ
मेरी वफ़ादारी ने तो मुझे कहीं का न छोड़ा है

दिल मेरा टूटा मगर, जाने दो मुझे क्या परवाह
तुम्हीं रहते थे इसमें, तुमने अपना ही मकाँ तोड़ा है

अफ़सोस यही है कि अब ज़िंदा क्यों नहीं हूँ आखिर
सुना है अब ज़माने ने मेरा नाम तुमसे जोड़ा है